G·A·L·A E·V·E·N·I·N·G

*You are cordially invited to our annual
Westminster roasting*

*In the presence of: Rt. Hon. Margaret Thatcher,
Rt. Hon. Neil Kinnock, Rt. Hon. David Steel,
Rt. Hon. David Owen and other distinguished guests.*

	Reception: 8.00 pm
	Dinner: 9.00 pm
R.S.V.P.	Carriages: 12.00

Dear

    O   h to be worthy

and l

of its   bian annual calendar of social events.

    As in past years, dinner will be followed by a number of
guest speakers from the world of politics and this year we
are celebrating our motto: "It is better to talk tripe than
to eat it". While other guest speakers will offer homage to
Lord Hailsham's speech in 1966 which has been a comfort and a
guiding light to so many of us:-

    "Politics should be fun, politicians have no right to be
dull or po-faced. The moment politics becomes dull,
democracy is in danger."

    We do hope that you will be able to join us on this
occasion and look forward to the pleasure of your company.

                    Yours truly

                    Adam Shaw
                    Hon. President

Acknowledgments

I am most grateful to all those who gave me permission to quote from their publications and to a number of people and organisations who have been especially kind in giving of their time and energy.

Acknowledgements in particular are due to the following: Thomas and Rita Shaw for their encouragement, Steve and Luca, The Conservative Party (Central Office), The Labour Party (Central Office, Edward Shirman), Nicolette Sorba for her invaluable work beyond the call of duty, *The Book of Political Quotations* by Jonathan Green, Angus 1982; *The Times*; *A Dictionary of Contemporary Quotations* compiled by Jonathan Green, David and Charles 1982; *Tories Broken Promises*, Labour Party Policy Directorate; *Political Quotes* by Michael Rogers, Sphere Books; *The Observer*; *Guide to Political Quotations* by C. Rathbone and M. Stephenson, Longman Pocket Companion 1985; *Dictionary of Political Quotations* by Robert Stewart, Penguin 1984; *The Soft Centre, The True Story of the SDP*, Labour Weekly Special Booklet; *South Wales Echo*; *Don't Quote Me* by Don Atyeo and Jonathan Green, Hamlyn Paperbacks 1981; *In Their Own Words – Key Tory Quotes*, Labour Party Research Department; *New Statesman*; *Breaking The Nation*, Labour Party Research Department; *The Sun*; *News of the World*; *Sunday Times*; *Cosmopolitan*; *Contradictory Quotations* by Michael Rogers, Longman; *Hansard*; *Times Educational Supplement*; *Conservative Manifesto 1979*; *Liberal News*; *Guardian*; *Scotsman*; *Morning Star*; *More Words for Eating* by Conservative Research Department; *Quote . . . Unquote* by Nigel Rees, Allen & Unwin 1978; *Conservative and Labour Party Conference Decisions 1945–81* Edited by F.W.S. Craig, Parliamentary Research Services; *Wolverhampton Express & Star*; *The Odyssey of Enoch – A Political Memoir* by Humphrey Berkley, Hamish Hamilton Ltd.; *Principles in Politics* by Roy Lewis, Castell Ltd.; *Daily Herald*; Diverse Reports, Quoted in *Breaking the Nation*, Channel 4; *Sunday Telegraph*; *Daily Mail*; *The Thatcher Government* by P. Riddell, Janus Robertson 1983; *Twentieth Century Quotations* by Frank S. Pepper, Sphere Reference 1987; *Daily Mirror*; *London Evening Standard*; *Parliamentary Profiles* by Roth; *Key Tory Quotes*; *Financial Times*; *Tory Quotes*, Labour Party Directorate; *Claret and Chips* by H. Stephenson, Michael Joseph 1982; *Inside the Alliance* by J. Joseph, John Martin 1983; *Daily News*; *City Limits*; *Guardian Weekly*; *Mail on Sunday*; *National Builder* journal of the Building Employers Confederation; *Daily Telegraph*; *New Socialist*; *Daily Express*.

Adam Shaw
London
April 1987

Political Rhubarb

by

ADAM SHAW

Ashford Press Publishing
Southampton
1987

Published by Ashford Press Publishing
1 Church Road
Shedfield
Hampshire
SO3 2HW

British Library Cataloguing in Publication Data

Political rhubarb.
  1. Politics, Practical —— Quotations,
maxims, etc.
  I. Shaw, Adam
  320   PN6084.P6

ISBN 1-85253-032-4

Designed and typeset by Jordan and Jordan, Fareham, Hampshire

Printed and bound in Great Britain by Robert Hartnoll (1985) Ltd., Bodmin, Cornwall

MENU

Starters: *A Little Taster*

Nonsense
Modesty is the Best Policy
All Work and No Play
Edwina Currie

Main Course: *Tripe and Onions*

Quote Unquote
Promises Promises
My Little Crystal Ball
Foot & Mouth Disease
I Beg to Differ
The Leisure Society
One For All and Every Man for Himself
Let's Have a Party
Of Cabbages and Kings

Dessert: *Gooseberry Fool*

Hot and Steamy
Sticks and Stones
Plus ça Change, Plus C'est la Même Chose
Last Words

STARTERS

A Little Taster

Nonsense

'You may call it "nonsense" if you like', she said,
'but I've heard nonsense compared with which
that would be as sensible as a dictionary.'
Lewis Carroll
The Jabberwocky

'A little nonsense now and then is not a bad thing –where would we Politicians be
if we were not allowed to talk it sometimes?'
Enoch Powell MP, 1965

Mr Enoch Powell, who refused to stand at the General Election, said last night on
the BBC Radio Programme Any Questions, that he had won the Election.
Times, 9/3/74

'It is tempting to deny, but if you deny you confirm what you won't deny, and by
confirming and denying you have announced before you have decided.'
Tony Benn MP, 1966

The Shi'ites are fighting against the Druze, the Druze and the Sunnis against the Shi'ites, comprising Amal and Hezbollah. The Prophets are battling against Karl Marx, the Communists against the Americans, and the Fundamentalists against the entire West.

A Beruit Newspaper, quoted in
The Times, 20/2/87

'I think that could be perhaps a little misleading and even our statistics can mislead people at times though they are not misleading in themselves. It is just that people get misled.'

Norman Tebbit MP, 14/3/84

'We need inequality to eliminate poverty.'

Sir Keith Joseph MP

'It needs to be said that the poor are poor because they don't have enough money.'
Sir Keith Joseph MP, 1970

'I would not say that the poor are poorer, except that they are more conscious of it.'

Indira Gandhi,
Observer, 1/8/82

'You don't tell deliberate lies, but sometimes you have to be evasive.'

Margaret Thatcher MP, 1976

'Some have lost or spent all their money. Others have lost their passports, their plane tickets and so on. Others have lost their cars, some don't know where they are and others are drunk.'

British Consulate Spokesman, Barcelona
On Scottish football fans
Observer, 28/5/72

'There are only three men who ever understood it; one was Prince Albert and he is dead, the second was a German Professor who became mad, I am the third and I've forgotten all about it.'

Lord Palmerston, 1863
On the Schleswig-Holstein Question

'Would it be right to understand that if there is a statement to be made, it will be made by Mr Heath and if there is no statement to be made it will be made by Mr Butler.'

Iain McLeod MP
Leader of the House of Commons

*Modesty is the
Best Policy*

'He hath indeed better bettered expectation than
you must expect of me to tell you how.'
Much Ado About Nothing.
Act I. Scene i.

'Oft expectation fails and most oft there where
most it promises, and oft it hits where hope is
coldest and despair most fits.'
Alls Well that Ends Well.
Act 2. Scene i.

'I don't think it will come for many many years, I don't think it will come in my lifetime.'

Margaret Thatcher MP
On the probability of a woman Prime Minister
BBC Radio, 14/1/72

'There has been a lot of talk about the formation of a new centre Party. Some have even been kind enough to suggest that I might lead it. I find this idea profoundly unattractive.'

Roy Jenkins MP

'At various times in the next twenty or thirty years I think it reasonable to anticipate that I will be among the Leadership of the Labour Party, but as far as being Leader, I can't see it happening and I'm not particularly keen on it happening.'

Neil Kinnock MP
South Wales Echo, 6/1/81

'The thought of being President frightens me and I do not think I want the job.'

Ronald Reagan, 1973

All Work
and No Play

'Play up, play up and play the game.'

'The Olympics will have the enthusiastic support of a Conservative Government.'

Hector Munro MP
Minister of Sport, 23/4/79

GOVERNMENT OLYMPIC
BOYCOTT DRIVE OPENS
Mr St John-Stevas (began) . . . a series of Ministerial speeches intended to persuade the British Olympic athletes to boycott the Moscow Games.

Times, 19/4/80

A glossy Soviet Olympic souvenir book . . . praises the attempts in 1936 to organise boycotts of the summer and winter Olympic games in Nazi Germany.

Times, 5/5/80

The USSR Olympic committee true to the ideals of the Olympic movement condemns the attempt at using sport as a means of political pressure

and calls upon . . . all people of good will to give a resolute rebuff to the sponsor of the present hostile campaign (to boycott the Games).

Times, 1/2/80

PROMISE OF NO COERCION OF ATHLETES

No 'oppressive methods', would be used to prevent athletes going to the Moscow Olympics . . .

Margaret Thatcher PM
Times, 5/1/80

SERVICEMEN BARRED FROM OLYMPIC GAMES

A ban on team events of British servicemen is likely to end the chance of a victory for the all-services pentathlon team.

The government . . . restricted the chances of civil servants and service personnel competing in the Olympic Games in Moscow by announcing that no special leave will be granted . . .

Times, 13/3/80

CURRIE CHIDES THE UNHEALTHY NORTH

Poor health among the people in the North of England was caused by ignorance, Mrs Edwina Currie . . . said yeaterday . . . she offered the South as an example of how people looked after themselves better.

Times, 24/9/86

'I won't claim the Workhouses didn't have their problems, but they were set up by people who cared.'

Edwina Currie MP
New Society, 3/10/86

'My message to the businessmen of this Country when they go abroad on business is that there is one thing above all they can take with them to stop them catching Aids – and that is the Wife.'

Edwina Currie MP
Guardian, 13/2/87

'I don't know what you get up to' she said laying a hand on my arm 'but it's hard to stop in the middle.'

Edwina Currie MP
On promoting sexual activities that stop short of intercourse,
New Society, 14/11/86

'Did the Prime Minister have some sort of grudge against you by sending this publicity crazed person into your Department.'

David Winnick MP
To Norman Fowler about Edwina Currie,
City Limits, 19-26/3/87

MAIN COURSE

Tripe and Onions

Quote Unquote

'I never deny, I never contradict, I
sometimes forget.'

Benjamin Disraeli
On dealing with Queen Victoria

'I feel a degree of regret that Marshall
did not push on and say 'abolish the
GLC' because I think it would have
been a major saving and would have
released massive resources for more
productive use.'

Ken Livingstone, 1979

'The idea that the GLC should be
abolished at a stroke is ill thought out,
undemocratic, and will cost the people
of London dear.'

Ken Livingstone
Times, 27/5/83

'We put a firm commitment to abolition in our Manifesto . . . and we are firmly commited to this course.'
Patrick Jenkins, MP, Dept. of Env. Press release about the abolition of the GLC, 21/9/83

Local Authorities should be given back responsibility for their own affairs in the face of 'increasing Government intervention.'
Patrick Jenkins MP New Statesmen, 22/11/86

'I do want to see a Parliament that is supreme.'
Ken Livingstone The Sun, 8/2/84

'I do not necessarily believe that we should give a blank cheque to the present majority in Parliament.'
Ken Livinstone The Sun, 8/2/84

'American nuclear weapons would almost certainly start being removed from Britian within 12 months of a Labour Government gaining power.'
Neil Kinnock MP Times, 3/10/86

Mr Kinnock . . . made clear that the removal of American bases plus weapons from Britain . . . will not be subject to a time limit.
Times, 18/3/87

'I must emphasise . . . that there is nothing in the Labour Party Constitution that could, or should, prevent people from holding opinions which favour Leninist-Trotskyism . . . Certainly Marxism . . . has, and will continue to have an important function in the Labour Party.'

Neil Kinnock MP
Broad Left Alliance Journal
October 1982

(He) delivered a stern warning that there was no place in the Labour Party for those obsessed with the 'Fringes and outer limits' of politics.

Neil Kinnock MP
Times, 25/6/85

'I couldn't live without work. That's what makes me so sympathetic towards these people who are unemployed. I don't know how they live without working.'

Margaret Thatcher PM
News of the World, 4/5/80

'Yes, I can give you examples of companies where employees have struck themselves out of jobs – and I say to them, don't blame your unemployment on me, it's your fault.'

Margaret Thatcher PM
Sunday Times, 5/5/81

'I hope we shall see more and more women combining marriage and a career. Prejudice against this dual role is not confined to men. Far too often, I regret to say, it comes from our own sex.'

Margaret Thatcher, 1952
Quoted in Cosmopolitan, May 1983

'We are not in politics to ignore peoples' worries, we are in politics to deal with them.'

Margaret Thatcher

Mrs. Margaret Thatcher (insisted) that it was sadly inevitable that there would have to be more unemployment.

Times, 25/6/80

'To accuse me of being too inflexible is poppycock.'

Margaret Thatcher PM
Observer, 1/11/81

'I remain totally convinced that when children are young, however busy we may be with the practical duties inside the home, the most important thing of all is to devote enough time and care to their needs and problems.'

Margaret Thatcher PM, 1982
Quoted in Cosmopolitan, May 1983

'Many of our troubles are due to the fact that our people turn to politicians for everything.'

Margaret Thatcher

'There is nothing inevitable about rising unemployment.'

Margaret Thatcher MP, 19/4/79

'I am extraordinarily patient, provided I get my own way in the end.'

Margaret Thatcher PM
Observer, 4/4/82

'The Labour Government likes to blame every ill and error on nameless World trends, in the face of which it is powerless.'

Margaret Thatcher MP, 1/5/79

'My Rt. Hon. Friend the Member for Stafford and Stone, gave an interesting speech demonstrating his concern for the young . . . a number of us feel that a compulsory project would not be right . . . If we were to have a compulsory project, we could not provide good facilities for all those who took part in it.'

Margaret Thatcher PM
Hansard, 24/6/81

Their (the Labour Party's) favourite excuse is that their appalling record is all due to the oil crisis and the World wide economic depression.

Conservative Manifesto, 1979

'It is a fact that 1980 was the year of the worst World economic recession since the 1930s. No British Government has had to face anything quite as bad as this for nearly 50 years.'

Margaret Thatcher PM, July 1982

The Prime Minister is heading for a clash . . . over the plan to deny all supplementary benefit to young people who refuse to join the Youth Training Scheme. . . . she said that young people under 18 should not be allowed to choose unemployment but should be made to take a job, stay in some form of education or go into training.

Times Educational Supplement
21/12/84

'When I first went to Downing Street, oil cost $14 a barrel. Now it is above $35 a barrel . . . so inevitably the demand for other things fell and unemployment rose.'

Margaret Thatcher, January 1982

'I am against any pact with the Nationalists because I am against pacts in principle.'

David Steel MP
Scotsman, 7/3/64

David Steel, one of the six Liberals surviving in the new Commons last night, proposed that the Liberals make electoral pacts with the Scottish and Welsh Nationalists.

Morning Star, 26/6/70

'This Government has no intention of giving into the current Protectionist clamour.'

Cecil Parkinson MP
Times, 11/4/80

'These duties, which have been secured as a result of British representation indicate the protection . . . (which) U.K. Industry can obtain. I believe this will be good news . . .'

Cecil Parkinson MP
Times, 21/5/81

'By the end of the next year, we really shall be on our way to that so-called economic miracle we need.'

> *Dennis Healey MP*
> *Ministerial Broadcast on the Budget*
> *6/4/76*

Sir Keith Joseph, Secretary of State for Education and Science has publicly admitted that . . . (there would be) a cut in the number of science and engineering places (at University).

> *Times, 10/12/81*

'If Britain becomes a member of the Community, it will be healthier for Britain, advantageous for Europe, and a gain for the whole World. I do not know of many economic or political problems in the World which will be easier to solve if Britain is outside rather than inside the Community.'

> *James Callaghan MP*
> *Chancellor of the Exchequer*
> *Hansard, 8/5/67*

'What I have always said is that no Government can produce an economic miracle.'

> *Dennis Healey MP*
> *BBC TV, 15/12/76*

Sir Keith Joseph . . . (complained) that technology teaching had virtually disappeared from the schools curriculum. He then made a plea for more girls to take science and technology subjects.

> *Times Educational Supplement, 16/9/83*

'Our conclusion in the Labour Party . . . is that we do not believe that the economic benefits of entry are sufficiently clear to justify the price that is asked.'

> *James Callaghan MP*
> *Shadow Foreign Sec.*
> *Hansard, 28/10/71*

'I myself have always deprecated, perhaps rightly, perhaps wrongly, in crisis after crisis, appeals to the Dunkirk spirit as an answer to our problem.'

Harold Wilson MP
Leader of the Opposition, 1961

'I believe that the spirit of Dunkirk will once again carry us through to success.'

Harold Wilson
Prime Minister, 1964.

'This conference congratulates the Government on the single-minded determination with which it has pursued the Price and Incomes Policy.'

Motion Carried
Labour Conference, 1966

'This conference declares its opposition to any . . . incomes policy designed to solve the problem of the economy by cutting the standard of living of workers.'

Motion Carried
Labour Conference, 1973

'Conference acknowledges that the safety of all people would best be served by multilateral disarmament in the nuclear and conventional fields.'

Motion Carried
Labour Conference, 1980

'This Conference instructs the NEC to ensure that the Manifesto includes an unambiguous commitment to unilateral disarmament.'

Motion Carried
Labour Conference, 1981

'I do not think that this would be the right moment to cut people's standard of life . . .'

James Callaghan PM
Hansard, 1/7/76

'Let me say that, of course, there has been a fall in people's standard of life . . . and (it) will fall again next year.'

James Callaghan PM
Panorama, 25/10/76

'The standard of living has been deliberately reduced by the Government over the last eighteen months . . . that should be a matter of congratulation and not for recrimination.'

Dennis Healey MP
ABC TV, 12/3/77

'Over the next three years . . . I think that public expenditure has got to come down as a proportion of the Gross Domestic Product.'

James Callaghan PM
Panorama, 25/10/76

'We're not foes of public expanditure. I want to see it increase.'

James Callaghan PM
Leeds, 4/12/76

'I have set and always will set my face like flint against making any difference between one citizen of this country and another on the grounds of his origin.'
Enoch Powell MP, 1964

'I supported as being right . . . the decision of Harold Macmillian to seek membership of the European Common Market.'
Enoch Powell MP
Clacton, 1969

'The West Indian or Asian does not, by being born in England, become an Englishman. In law, he becomes a United Kingdom citizen by birth. In fact, he is a West Indian or Asian still.'
Enoch Powell MP, 1968

'Those candidates, and only those candidates ought to receive our vote at the next General Election who are individually committed . . . to vote on all subjects in such a way as to terminate Britain's present membership of the community.'
Enoch Powell MP, Speech to the
Safeguard Britain Campaign Meeting
Westminster, 3/6/78

'The country has a right to hear from the P.M. whether she and the Government envisage the official figure rising to that total.'
Michael Foot – asking Margaret
Thatcher to predict whether
unemployment would reach the
3 million level, Hansard, 24/6/81

'No, I shall not make such a prediction. It would not be sensible. Indeed, I do not think that any Government has made predictions of the character suggested'.
Michael Foot refusing to predict
unemployment levels.
Hansard, 28/10/75

'I've never made an inflammatory
statement in my life.'
            Rev. Ian Paisley MP, 1969

'Lewd, immoral, foul-mouthed,
drunken M.Ps mouthing about Ulster.'
            Rev. Ian Paisley MP
            The Sun, 11/5/77

'There was no impropriety whatsoever
in my acquaintance with Miss Keeler.'
            John Profumo MP

'I said there had been no impropriety …
that was not true and I misled you, and
my colleagues and the House.'
            John Profumo MP
            Daily Herald, 23/3/63

'For the first time we have seen the
Police having to resort to some kind of
paramilitary style of policing, which we
have always prided ourselves on having
avoided …'
            John Alderton
            Former Chief Constable of Devon &
            Cornwall Diverse Reports, 17/10/84

'We are prepared to shoot and kill in the
interest of society.'

            John Alderton
            Former Chief Constable of
            Devon & Cornwall
            Observer, 25/2/79

'The discovery of the nuclear chain reactions need not bring about the destruction of mankind any more than did the discovery of matches.'

Albert Einstein, 1952

'The release of atom power has changed everything but our ways of thinking and thus we are being driven, unarmed, towards catastrophe.'

Albert Einstein, 1946

Promises Promises

'A Manifesto is issued to get votes and is not to be taken as the Gospel.'
Lord Denning
Observer, 15/11/81

No plans have been prepared to make compulsory the use of secret ballot . . . the choice of whether to have a ballot will be left to the individual unions.
Conservative Plans
Sunday Telegraph, 6/5/79

The Trade Union Bill . . . introduces compulsory secret ballots . . .
Times, 27/10/83

'No one should think that if our mates are in trouble in the mining industry the TUC will stand by with its arms folded.'
Len Murray, TUC General Secretary
Observer, 3/2/74

'As far as relations with the TUC and Union leaders are concerned, Conservative Ministers would discuss and consult with them . . . no topic would be barred from discussion.'
James Prior MP
Times, 16/3/77

Mr. Scargill attacked the TUC General Council for failing to provide 'desperately needed financial assistance' to the union in the wake of its sequestration and receivership.
Times, 2/7/85

GIVE UNIONS A SAY URGES MURRAY
'If the Government turns a deaf ear . . . Trade Unions cannot simply shut shop.'
Len Murray
Daily Telegraph, 25/9/79

'We shall put it to the Chancellor: "Do you really want consultation? Or do you want consultation to be Ministers meeting the TUC after government decisions have been taken." '
Len Murray
Daily Telegraph, 26/7/79

We shall cut income tax at all levels.
Conservative Manifesto, 1979

Mrs. Thatcher dismissed what she described as Labour 'smears' – that a Conservative government would double VAT.

Daily Telegraph, 24/4/79

'There is no commitment whatsoever to abolish the price commission.'
Francis Pym MP
Panorama, 23/4/79

'Pressimists say that we can never solve unemployment. They are wrong and I intend to prove it.'
Norman Tebbit MP, 7/8/82

'We have had over the past four years to increase the level of taxation overall.'
Nigel Lawson MP
Financial Times, 7/9/83

VAT UP TO ONE STANDARD RATE OF 15%, FROM . . . 8%
Daily Mail, 13/6/79

The Price Commission (is) to be scrapped. The formal announcement about the expected abolition . . . was made by Mr. Nott, Trade Secretary last night.

Daily Telegraph, 16/5/79

1982 : 2,700,000 UNEMPLOYED
1986 : 3,500,000 UNEMPLOYED
New Statesman, August 1986

'We should see to it that our people are steeped in a real knowledge and understanding of our National culture.'
Margaret Thatcher PM
May 1980

Seven members of the Art Council drama panel resigned yesterday . . . (accusing) the Arts Council of 'betraying the arts by acquiesing to government policy.' Last month they called on the Council to say publically that the cuts . . . would make its entire drama strategy unworkable.
Times, 1/3/85

We must restore to every child, regardless of background, the chance to progress as his or her abilities allow.
Conservative Manifesto, 1979

'I think I am presiding at the moment over an education system in which there really is inadequate provision for a very substantial minority.'
Sir Keith Joseph MP
Minister for Education, 20/2/83

Our goal is to make Britain the best housed Nation in Europe.
Conservative Manifesto 1983

'Since Mrs. Thatcher first gained office . . . we have seen truely massive cuts in our capital construction programmes, a serious reduction in housing opportunities . . .'
President of Building Employers Confederation, National Builder, June 1984

'Send us the bills and we will pay them.'

Edwina Currie MP
Under-Secretary Dept. of Health
Times, 15/1/87

Yesterday (Edwina Currie) personally backed a new report from the British Cardiac Society on heart disease . . . unfortunately the DHSS cannot afford the £600 to buy the reports from the charity, which must instead foot the bill for keeping our elected representatives in the know.

Times, 12/2/87

'Let me make it clear: the Conservative Party has no plans for new NHS charges.'

Margaret Thatcher PM
Tory Press Conference, 18/4/79

Precription charges are to go up from 45p to 70p from next April – the second increase in a year.

Daily Telegraph, 2/11/79

'The Conservatives will be saving public expenditure not increasing it.'
Sir Geoffrey Howe MP, 24/4/79

We . . . note the consistent & significant rise in expanditure for the period to date . . .

Treasury & Civil Service
Committee of the Commons
March 1983

My Little Crystal Ball

'I'll never get married again.'
Liz Taylor
(seven times married)
Observer, 28/2/82

'Within a decade no child will go to bed hungry . . .'
Henry Kissenger
World Food Conference, 1974

'A child squatting in its own diarrhoea and it has nothing left to shit except its own stomach . . . they wake up, start using calories, and they die.'
Bob Geldof
Guardian, 17/1/85

'I fear that within ten years . . . gays, Trade Union activists and Left wing Politicians will be led off to the gas chambers.'

Ken Livingstone
Observer, 23/8/81

'The Task Force . . . will cost this Country a far greater humiliation than we have already suffered . . . the attempt will fail.'

Tony Benn MP
House of Commons, 7/4/82

'Its is inconceivable for Labour to lose this election.'

James Callaghan PM
Daily Telegraph, 5/5/79

'I foresee a Liberal vote so massive and the number of Liberal MPs so great that we shall hold the initiative in the new Parliament.'

David Steel MP Observer, 14/9/80

A Tory Council leader said yeaterday that the way to stamp out Aids was by "putting 90% of homosexuals in the gas chamber."

Bill Brownhill, Cllr.
Guardian, 18/12/86

VICTORY IN SIGHT
British troops were storming towards Falklands victory last night as the Argies fled in disarray.

Sun, 15/6/82

Mrs Thatcher has won a clear victory … she should get the credit for their triumph.

Daily Mirror, 5/5/79

GENERAL ELECTION RESULTS

Conservatives	397
Labour	209
Liberal	17

Times, 11/6/83

'It is quite clear to me that the Tory Party will get rid of Mrs Thatcher in about 3 years time.'

Sir Harold Wilson
23/11/80

'I see no reason why the mass of British business should find itself short of money for investment in the coming year.'

Denis Healey MP
Hansard, 1/4/74

'The Social Contract is our answer – in the short term, the medium & the long term to the problems of a modern industrialised society.'

Sir Harold Wilson
Bury, 26/9/74

'There are going to be no dramatic changes in Rhodesia'

Ian Smith
Observer, 5/1/79

1975: Thatcher elected as Leader of theConservative Party.
1987: Thatcher still leader of the Conservative Party.

'Thousands of private companies are so short of cash that they are already beginning to lay off workers . . .'

Dennis Healey MP
Labour Party Conference, 29/11/74

Mr Callaghan was forced to admit in the Commons that the Social Contract could no longer be considered intact or sound.

Times, 8/7/77

SMITH HANDS OVER AS
ZIMBABWE IS BORN
Eighty-nine years of white rule ended and the new era of black rule began . . .
Daily Telegraph, 1/6/79

'I have spent 6 days in Argentina . . . a country with a warm friendship towards Britain . . . I return to London . . . convinced that during the 1980s both countries . . . will benefit from the new spirit of collaboration.'

Mr P. Walker MP
25/9/80

HIGH NOON

Britain set to shoot Argies out of sky. War with Argentina looks like starting tomorrow.

Sun, 29/4/82

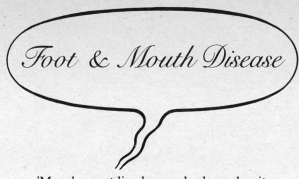

Foot & Mouth Disease

'Man does not live by words alone, despite
the fact that sometimes he must eat them.'
Adlai Stevenson

'People can say what they want in the
Labour Party.'

Michael Foot MP
Observer, 25/1/81

Mr. Michael Foot . . . made plain . . .
that he expects the eight local Labour
Parties which have chosen Militant
parliamentary candidates to drop them
unless they renounce their Trotskyite
allegiance.

Times, 13/9/82

FOOT DISOWNS LEFT WING CANDIDATE

Mr Micheal Foot (said) . . . he would do all in his power to block the endorsement of . . . hard left prospective parliamentary candidate Mr. Peter Tatchell.

Times, 4/12/81

'I've never been in favour of expelling people from the Labour Party . . .'
Michael Foot MP
Sun, 20/1/81

'I cannot vote for Denis Healey for a leading position in the Party. He is on the right I am on the left.'
Neil Kinnock MP
Tribune, 18/9/81

Mr. Michael Foot . . . yesterday posed for photographs at Westminster with Peter Tatchell, the official Labour candidate . . .
Times, 15/2/83

Tony Benn . . . is . . . to oppose Foot's plan to rid Labour of Militant by excluding it from the register of permitted organisations which the Party is currently setting up.
Sunday Times, 25/7/82

Nearly all the top posts in the Neil Kinnock Shadow Cabinet . . . are to go to figures on the Centre-Right of the Labour Party . . . Mr Denis Healey will remain Shadow Foreign Secretary.
Times, 31/10/83

'By any measure of political, civil, Trade Union or human rights, the Gadaffy regime is vile. Any offers from them would be an insult to everything the British Trade Union movement stands for. If such offers are ever made, then of course they must be rejected.'

Neil Kinnock MP, Guardian, 29/10/84

PARTY LIVES BY LEGALITY
'We cannot sharpen legality as our main weapon for the future and then simultaneously scorn legality because it does not suit us at the present time.'

Neil Kinnock MP, Times, 3/10/84

Mr Winsor – NUM Chief Executive – (said) . . . 'We need all the money you can send us through the Libyan Trade Unions.' Colonel Gadaffy replied . . . 'I can confirm that the Libyan Trade Unions will contribute substantial cash . . .'

Times, 3/11/84

LABOUR VOTES TO SUPPORT ILLEGAL COUNCIL SPENDING
Labour Party Conference
Times, 4/10/84

'To suggest that the Conservative Party would seek to be in conflict with the Trade Unions is to suggest that we are in favour of cutting off one of our own limbs.'

James Prior MP, 1978

TORY PLAN 'BLUEPRINT FOR INDUSTRIAL CIVIL WAR'
Sir Keith Joseph . . . confirmed yesterday that the Tories are considering sweeping plans to break up the nationalised industries and ways to beat the unions if there should be another confrontation.

Sunday Times, 28/5/78

New Employment Supremo, Tom King will warn union Chiefs today: 'I can be as nasty as Norman.'

On Norman Tebbit MP
Sun, 19/10/83

Battling Premier Margaret Thatcher . . . pledged to clip the wings of Britain's Unions.

Sun, 29/2/80

'Politicians are either warriors or healers, Margaret Thatcher is a healer.'

P. Cosgrave, Biographer

'If someone is confronting our essential liberties, if someone is inflicting injuries and harm – by God I'll confront them.'

Margaret Thatcher PM, 1979

'I've never bashed a union in my life.'
Norman Tebbit MP
Observer, 18/10/81

(Norman Tebbit) said it was anti-libertarian to ban the closed shop.
October 1977

'If there is any emergence of a fourth Party in British politics, it is the task of the Liberal Party to strangle it at birth.'
Cyril Smith MP
Observer, 18/1/81

'There has been no pressure by the Prime Minister's office, nor by any other government office, about the search warrant used by the Police in their search of BBC offices in Glasgow.'
Mr. P. Fraser
Solicitor-General for Scotland.
Times, 12/2/87

The tough, brooding, relentless union-bashing image of Employment Secretary Norman Tebbit brought the Tories to their feet.
Daily Mirror, 14/10/83

TORIES BAN CLOSED SHOP
London Evening Standard , 24/2/87

Mr Smith said he wanted to make it clear that he supported the Alliance . . .
Guardian, 16/9/81

TORY PEER ADMITS BBC RAID DIRECTION
The Senior Scottish law Advocate . . . revealed details of his supervision of the warrants used in the . . . raid on the BBC.
Guardian, 5/2/87

'Our problem at the moment is a problem of success.'
Edward Heath PM, 1973

Now Wilson and Heath both firmly declare that the final decision . . . must be made by government . . . they reject the idea of a National referendum.
On entry into the Common Market.
Daily Mirror, 3/6/70

'Only a fool wants a confrontation and only a fool wants a strike.'
Arthur Scargill President of the National Union of Mineworkers
Observer, 6/11/77

HEATH QUITS . . .
Tory Leader, Edward Heath, who lost at the polls, went to Buckingham Palace . . . to offer his resignation.
Sun, 5/3/74

Premier Harold Wilson announced that a referendum on Britain's membership will be held, probably before the end of June.
Daily Mirror, 24/1/75

On March 12th 1984, Arthur Scargill called 55,000 Yorkshire miners out on a strike. Within a fortnight the number had doubled. During the year long strike two miners died while on picket line 1,391 police officers were injured, the NUM was fined £200,000 and had its funds seized, 38 coalfaces were lost and the Country footed a bill of £3.3 billion. On March 5th 1985 the strike was called off not having won its declared objectives.
Information from the Guardian, 5/3/85

I Beg to Differ

'All government . . . is
founded on compromise
& banter.'
Edmund Burke

'He got on his bike and looked for
work and he kept looking until he found
it.'

Norman Tebbit MP on his father
Tory Party Conference, 1981

'thus it would be wrong to suppose that
a higher level of mobility would lead to
a major reduction in unemployment.'

Lord Young
Employment Secretary, 8/11/86

'I wonder, whether insider dealing . . . is such an abuse as is supposed by my Rt. Hon. and Hon. gentlemen. It could have some beneficial effects.'

Nicholas Ridley MP
Hansard, 17/1/74

'With the co-operation of industry, commerce and government we are all in a very much more competitive position than we were before.'

Margaret Thatcher PM
Sunday Telegraph, 14/2/82

'I understand very well, we all understand very well, just how the shadow of unemployment brings wretchedness and despair to entire communities.'

Sir Geoffrey Howe MP
BBC TV, 15/10/80

'Only one year after the Conservative government came to office, insider dealing became a criminal offence. That shows that we put it at the top of our list while the Labour Party put it at the bottom.'

Paul Channon MP
Hansard, 28/1/87

'Across whole areas of manufacturing, the loss of a competitive edge has meant the loss of World markets which in some cases it is scarcely possible to see us getting back.'

Sir Francis Pym MP
Times, 3/2/82

'The high level of unemployment is evidence of the progress we are making.'

Nicholas Ridley MP, 26/1/81

The Leisure Society

'The Government's policies are
designed to bring unemployment down.'
Sir Geoffrey Howe MP

1980: UNEMPLOYMENT AT 1,665,000
'We are reaching the trough of the recession and it will start to turn towards the end
of next year.'

Margaret Thatcher PM
Financial Times, 26/11/80

1981: UNEMPLOYMENT AT 2,520,000

'We are at the end of the recession.'

Sir Geoffrey Howe MP
Observer, 2/8/81

1982: UNEMPLOYMENT AT 2,917,000

'The evidence of the start of the recovery is all about us. Not even the most blinkered pessimist could fail to see it.'

Leon Brittan MP, May 1982

1983: UNEMPLOYMENT AT 3,105,000

'There is every prospect that by next year we will see the start of a fall in the level of unemployment.'

Nigel Lawson MP
Guardian, 21/5/83

1986: UNEMPLOYMENT AT 3,500,000

'If unemployment is not below 3,000,000 in five years, then I'm not worth re-electing.'

Norman Tebbit MP, 17/5/83

One For All and Every Man For Himself

'A song for Our Banner the Watchword recall,
United we stand, divided we fall.'

'The Labour Party can go into the next election united behind the most radical manifesto on which we have ever campaigned.'

Roy Hattersley MP
New Socialist, March 1983

A split on nuclear defence between Michael Foot and Denis Healey plunged Labour's election strategy into chaos yesterday.

Sun, 25/5/83

Former Labour Prime Minister Jim Callaghan made a furious attack on his own Party's defence policy last night.

Sun , 26/5/83

Labour's Manifesto states unequivocally that Labour will get rid of all nuclear weapons (but) . . . Denis Healey, Roy Hattersley, and Peter Shore are now telling us that British nuclear disarmament will depend on . . . concessions out of the Russians . . . No wonder the public is confused about Labour's defence policy when half the Shadow Cabinet appear not to understand it either.

Tribune, 27/5/83

The SDP Liberal Alliance is more united . . . than the (Tories) . . . or the . . . Labour Party 'We solved the problem of how to get two parties to work closely together for the first time in modern British politics.'

Mr. Alan Beith MP
Acting Liberal Leader, Times, 13/9/83

A CLUTCH OF RED FACES FOR DISUNITED ALLIANCE.
. . . At the very moment when Dr. David Owen & Mr. David Steel were . . . proclaiming Alliance unity they were voting in separate lobbies at Westminster.

Times, 30/1/87

Mr. Jenkins said . . . an Alliance government could maintain 'our independent deterrent for a substantial period ahead.'

Times, 9/6/83

'Liberals have always opposed the concept of an independent nuclear deterrent.'

David Steel MP
Times, 8/6/83

Let's Have a Party

'The art of being a good guest is to know when to leave.'
Prince Philip

'The most foolish course now for those
who are determined to swing the Party
back to sensible Socialism, would be to
abandon the struggle within the Party,
to talk of forming new Parties.'
David Owen MP, 1975

'The most moving speech I ever heard was Hugh Gaitskill saying he would 'fight, fight and fight again to save the Party we love.' That was the right message in 1960, and I believe it is still the right message today.'

Roy Jenkins MP

'I am not interested in a third Party. I do not believe it has any future.'

Shirley Williams MP, 25/5/80

On March 27th 1981 the Social Democratic Party was formed. Its founding members were: David Owen MP, Roy Jenkins MP, Shirley Williams MP and William Rodgers MP.

'The danger of any new Party at a time of disillusion with the old Parties, is that it becomes all things to all men.'

Shirley Williams MP, Observer, 29/3/81

'The only thing that isn't in it is being kind to animals.'

Denis Healey MP
On SDP Programme
Observer, 29/3/81

Mr David Crouch (Canterbury):
'On a point of order Mr Speaker in your determination of who should speak . . . did you choose the Rt.Hon. Member for Roxburgh, Selkirk and Peebles (Mr Steel) as the Leader of the Liberal Party or as the Leader of the Liberal Party in Alliance with the SDP?'

Mr Speaker:
'There are some secrets which I keep to myself because I want to stay alive.'

Of Cabbages and Kings

'The time has come', the Walrus said, 'to talk of many things. Of shoes and ships and sealing wax, of cabbages and Kings.'

Lewis Carroll

BONGO BONGO MP IN RACE FURY

Premier Margaret Thatcher faced demands last night to sack a Minister alleged to have referred to Britain's Blacks as coming from "Bongo Bongo Land". Furious Labour MPs insisted that Alan Clark, Employment Junior Minister responsible for Race Relations was unfit for Office.

Daily Mirror, 7/2/85

'I shall present this code to Parliament like a Head waiter obliged to pour a glass of Coca-Cola.'

Norman Tebbit MP
On the Code of the employment of ethnic minorities.
Mail on Sunday, 21/11/82

'I personally feel very undecided whether it is better for a woman to stay and look after the home or go out to a job.'

Sir Geoffrey Howe MP
Morning Star, 26/11/86

'If the good Lord had intended us to have equal rights to go out to work, he wouldn't have created Man and Woman.'

Partick Jenkin MP
Man Alive, 30/10/79

'People can clean their teeth in the dark.'

Patrick Jenkin MP
On his solution to the Energy Crisis
Times, 16/1/74

'When MPs visit you please remember at least to offer to feed them.'

Cyril Smith MP
Observer, 4/5/75

'Will (he) review the arrangement for preventing drowning accidents?'
John Stonehouse MP
Question in the House of Commons
7/5/75

Former British Cabinet Minister, Mr. John Stonehouse is believed to have drowned in waters off Miami yesterday . . . A Police spokesman said Mr Stonehouse was last seen swimming at Fontainebleau's private beach.
Daily Mail, 22/11/74

'Britain has invented a new Missile. It's called the Civil Servant – it doesn't work and it can't be fired.'

General Sir Walter Walker
Observer, 15/3/81

'The Prime Minister is stealing our clothes but he is going to look pretty ridiculous walking around in mine.'

Margaret Thatcher MP, 1973

TORY MP SLAPS A MINISTER

A Minister was hit across the face with a Commons paper last night. The blow came from a Tory MP . . . Suddenly Mr Lawson's Order paper . . . struck Mr Davis across the face . . . Party colleagues then put calming arms around their shoulders and led them away.

Daily Mirror, 5/3/75

FROM AROUND THE WORLD

'We are looking for a Wealth Tax that will bring in sufficient revenue to justify having a Wealth Tax.'

Dick Spring
Leader of the Irish Labour Party
Observer, 5/12/82

'We Germans, who are the only people in the World who have a decent attitude towards animals, will also assume a decent attitude towards these Human animals.'

Henrich Himmler
Head of SS, 4/10/43

'Let us begin by committing ourselves to the truth, to see it like it is, and to tell it like it is, to find the truth, to speak the truth and to live with the truth. That's what we'll do.'

President Nixon, 1968

'Government is like a baby. An alimentary canal with a big appetite at one end and no sense of responsibility at the other.'

Ronald Reagan
Saturday Evening Post, 1965

'My basic rule is that I want people who don't want a job in government.'

Ronald Reagan
President-elect
Observer, 16/11/80

'You can tell a lot about a Fellow's character by the way he eats Jelly Beans.'

President Reagan
Observer, 25/1/81

'My fellow Americans, I am pleased to tell you that I have signed legislation to outlaw Russia forever. We begin bombing in five minutes.'

President Reagan
Testing a Microphone, unaware he was being recorded.
11/8/84

(The Tower Report) establishes that the President was present at regular briefings about the operation though it concedes that he never appeared to pay close attention to what was going on.

On President Reagan and the 'Irangate' controversy
Daily News, 26/2/87

DESSERT

Gooseberry Fool

Hot and Steamy

'Sex is like having dinner, sometimes you joke about the dishes, sometimes you take the meal seriously.'
Woody Allen

'We are a Party of the highest morals.'
Peter Bruinvels MP
Times, 27/10/86

ADULTERER AND A DAMNED FOOL – MPs ATTACK ON CECIL
On Cecil Parkinson's affair with Sara Keays
Sun, 12/10/83

In 1963 Mr. J Profumo . . . was forced to resign from the House of Commons over his associations with prostitute Christine Keeler.

Times, 27/10/86

'As a Conservative Party we do not deal with prostitutes . . . no deals must ever be made with people of dubious character.'

Peter Bruinvels MP
Times, 27/10/86

Yesterday, Lord Jellicoe, Leader of the House of Lords, joined RAF Minister Lord Lambton in resigning over affairs with Call girls.

Sun, 25/5/73

One of the main characters in Jeffrey Archer's recent novel 'First Among Equals' was caught by a prostitute. Raymond Gould survived the resulting blackmail, Mr. Archer was not so fortunate.

Times, 27/10/86

THEY ALL DO IT, SAYS MP

A top-drawer Tory last night launched an amazing defence of unfaithful MP Winston Churchill – by claiming that all leading Politicians have had affairs.

Sun, 17/12/79

President Mitterand of France remarked during one recent sex scandal in British Politics that if he were forced to restrict the formation of his government to those who had never had extra-marital affairs or been known to indulge sexual peccadilloes, then his choice would be restricted to some forty homosexuals.

Times, 27/10/86

The Conservative 'cowardly approach' to the Common Market would earn them no more than 'a French kiss and a German hug.'

John Silkin MP
Daily Telegraph, 3/5/79

'It's time for the kissing to stop and the negotiating to start.'

Richard Holme
Calling on David Owen and other to
"get on with their revolt."Sunday Times, 5/2/81

'We have of course often done it before, but never on a pavement outside a hotel in Eastbourne. We have done it in various rooms in one way or another at various functions. It is perfectly genuine and normal – and normal and right – so to do.'

William Whitelaw
On kissing Margaret Thatcher

'Rape is a crime I've never been forced to commit.'

Nicholas Fairbairn MP
Guardian, 22/1/82

'A gentleman who for reasons of chivalry I shall not mention but who occupied grand office and who had taken grandly of wine and allowed veritas to overcome him, went up to the Prime Minister and . . . told her that he had always fancied her, to which the Prime Minister replied, "Quite right: you have very good taste but I just don't think you would make it at the moment."'

Nicholas Fairbairn MP
Hansard, 14/1/85

'I must tell my Hon. friend (Miss Janet Fookes MP) . . . that although I have always been attracted to her I have never actually dared ask her whether she would go to bed with me . . .'

Nicholas Fairbairn MP
Hansard, 25/1/85

'All the poison that my Hon. friend (Edwina Currie) suggests I would happily take rather than be spread eagled on the floor of the House by her.'

Nicholas Fairbairn MP
Hansard, 14/1/85

'. . . nobody is fonder of women than I am.'

Nicholas Fairbairn MP
Guardian, 22/1/82

Mr Fairbairn: Hon. Members who were in the army will remember that the fourth Halogen, Bromide, was added to tea, called number nine, to reduce the sex urge.

Mr. Craigen: It didn't do the Hon. and learned gentleman any good.

Hansard, 14/1/85

James Prior: If you put a bull in a field with a herd of cows you wouldn't expect to see a lot of calfs the next morning.

James Callaghan: No, but you'd except to see a lot of contented faces.

SEX RULING

The vatican in a policy document tomorrow, is expected to brand test-tube babies as immoral, and to allow condoms to be used if they have a small hole.

Guardian, 9/3/87

Sticks and Stones

'You should learn not to make personal remarks' said Alice to the Mad Hatter.
Lewis Carroll

'The trouble with the Socialist Worker's Party is that they live in an historical thermos-flask.'

Neil Kinnock MP
Daily Telegraph, 11/10/84

'They travel best in gangs, hanging around like clumps of bananas, thick skinned and yellow.'

Neil Kinnock MP
On the Tories
Observer, 22/2/87

'It behaves more like a Tribe than a democratic institution . . . responding to custom rather than reason and using its own liturgy and language for the conduct of its domestic affairs.'

Christopher Patten MP
On the Conservative Party
Times, 10/10/81

'A good man fallen among Politicians'

Leader Comment on Michael Foot MP
Daily Mirror, 20/2/83

'Unless the Country sees evidence soon . . . of (Michael Foot's) willingness to stand firm . . . he will go down in history as Mr Pussy Foot.'

Cyril Smith MP
Hansard, 3/10/74

'Like being savaged by a dead sheep.'

Denis Healey MP
on Geoffrey Howe MP
14/6/78

'Like being nuzzled by an old Ram.'

Geoffrey Howe MP
on Denis Healey MP
28/6/83

'Couldn't knock the skin off a rice pudding.'

Neil Kinnock MP on Tony Benn MP
Mail on Sunday, 25/9/83

'Wilson is a petty bourgeois and will remain so in spirit even if they make him a Viscount.'

Neil Kinnock MP
Mail on Sunday, 25/9/83

'A timid old Tory.'

Barbara Castle MP on James Callaghan MP
Daily Mirror, 18/9/80

'Paisley has been and remains a greater threat to the Union than the Foreign Office and the Provisional IRA rolled into one.'

Enoch Powell MP
Observer, 11/1/81

'Arthur Scargill is the Labour movement's nearest equivalent to a First World War General.'

Neil Kinnock MP
Channel 4, 9/9/84

'Arthur Scargill is a bloody lunatic.'

Neil Kinnock MP
Sounds, 15/10/83

'He's arrogant, orthopaedically arrogant in every corpuscle.'
Neil Kinnock MP on David Owen MP
Mail on Sunday, 25/9/83

THE OTHER UNFORTUNATES

Mr Eric Varley . . . (said) putting Mr Norman Tebbit in charge of employment 'was like putting Dracula in charge of a blood transfusion service.'
Times, 21/5/83

'Dr Strangelove of the Economic World.'
James Callaghan MP on Sir Keith Joseph MP
Daily Telegraph, 16/5/79

'A loutish Minister of the Thuggish tendency.'
Michael Meacher MP on Norman Tebbit MP
Morning Star, 28/7/86

'It would be excellent if he is prepared to listen to other points of view.'
Shirley Williams MP on David Owen MP
Daily Mail, 9/6/86

'She puts on a Fish wife act, always screaming away with her face absolutely contorted.'

Gerald Kaufman MP
Mail on Sunday, 22/2/87

'This woman is headstrong, obstinate and dangerously self-opinionated.'
Report on Thatcher by Personnel Office at ICA after rejecting her for a job.
1948

'I am a great admirer of Mrs Thatcher – one of the most splendid Headmistresses there has ever been.'

Arthur Marshall
BBC Radio 4, 22/1/82

'I have a vision of her at the end of the century looking like the late Queen Victoria . . . still there, and having become a National institution.'

Norman Tebbit MP
Daily Telegraph, 9/10/84

A ROSE BY ANY OTHER NAME

POOR MRS T!

'She is bounder, a liar, a deceiver a cheat, a crook and a disgrace to the House of Commons.'

Tam Dayell MP
Mail on Sunday, 22/2/87

'On behalf of the People of Ulster, I brand you a Traitor and a liar.'

Rev. Ian Paisley MP
Mail on Sunday, 22/2/87

'Plunder Woman'

Harry Urwin
Chairman of the Employment Policy
and Organisation Comittees.
Times, 2/9/80

'Mrs Thatcher may be a woman but she isn't a sister.'

Feminist Writer
Observer, 7/10/79

'. . . the American lacky.'

Colonel Gadaffy
Times, 3/11/84

'My only great qualification for being put in charge of the Navy is that I am very much at sea.'

Ed Carson
First Lord Of Admiralty
December 1916

'It was amazing that I was ever elected.'

Rev. Ian Paisley, MP
City Limits, 19-26/3/87

'I would have made a good Pope.'

Richard Nixon
Ex-USA President.

'Without false modesty, I don't think that I have a fraction of the talent of either Bevan or Foot.'

Neil Kinnock MP
South Wales Echo, 6/1/81

As the Prime Minister (James Callaghan) put it to me . . . he saw his role being that of Moses.

Guardian Weekly, 18/9/77

'(I) would quite like to be a nice Liberal version of Norman Tebbit.'
Mathew Taylor, Liberal Candidate, Truro by-election
Before becoming the youngest MP in the Commons
Observer, 22/2/87

'I am an optimist, but I am an optimist who takes his raincoat.'

Harold Wilson

'I'm no ghost.'

James Callaghan, MP
Observer, 8/6/80

'I have never been an idealist – that implies you aren't going to achieve something.'
Arthur Scargill,
NUM President, 1974

'ME, A NAME I CALL MYSELF'

'Yes I am a virus – I am the virus that kills Socialists.'

Enoch Powell, MP
Daily Telegraph, 2/10/68

'I am on the right wing of the middle of the road with a strong radical bias.'

Tony Benn MP, 1950s

'If the fence is strong enough I'll sit on it.'

Cyril Smith, MP

'I'm still a loony, dribbling Leftie.'

Ken Livingstone
Sun, 10/7/85

'A good solid middle of the road Conservative like me.'

Norman Tebbit, MP
Times, 7/2/87

Plus ça Change,
Plus C'est la Même Chose

'It will all be the same a hundred years hence.'
Proverb

'An Ambassador is an honest man sent abroad to lie for the Commonwealth.'
Sir Henry Wotton, 1604

(Sir Robert Armstrong) was the 'Classic fall guy . . . a man sent abroad to lie for his Country.'
Times, 18/12/86

'Women never reason and therefore they are (comparatively) seldom wrong.'
William Hazlitt, 1823

'I usually make my mind up about a man in ten seconds and I very rarely change it.'
Margaret Thatcher MP, 1970

'If they have no bread, let them eat cake.'

Marie-Antoinette, 1780s

TORY MOTHER'S ADVICE TO
JOBLESS
LET THEM EAT PORRIDGE
Dr. Nonny Tiffany, a City councillor said "When you are broke eat porridge and go for long walks in the Countryside . . . You can live on porridge for a long time . . . I was out of a job myself for six months and porridge was certainly on my diet.'

Daily Mirror, 3/8/85

A POSTSCRIPT

Tory Councillor, Dr. Nonny Tiffany . . . has had her house at Oxford daubed with porridge and the letters PLO standing for 'Porridge Liberation Organisation' – in red paint.

New Statesman, 6/9/85

CRISIS? WHAT CRISIS?
Sun tanned Premier Jim Callaghan breezed back into Britain yesterday and asked 'Crisis? What Crisis?'

Sun, 11/1/79

The Crisis is here.
The Ostrich Prime Minister must be made to face it as the rest of us have to.

Daily Mail, 11/1/79

70

'Crisis? What crisis? There is no crisis.'

Nigel Lawson MP
Times, 19/8/84

'With regard to opinion in the Thatcher household, the Prime minister does not have a monopoly.'

Margaret Thatcher PM
Observer, 20/1/80

'Most of our people have never had it so good.'

Harold Macmillan
Bradford, 20/7/57

'Democracy means government by discussion, but it is only effective if you can stop people talking.'

Clement Atlee, 1962

Premier Margaret Thatcher flew back from holiday yesterday to grapple with the growing industrial crisis.

Daily Mirror, 28/8/84

'The Labour Party is being led by a woman but she has not been elected to anything. She is the lady who makes the breakfast in the Kinnock household.'

Edwina Currie MP
Observer, 22/2/87

'The country has never had so good a time as it has today . . . for the 87% of us who are working.'

Lord Young
TV AM, May 1986

'I don't mind how much my Ministers talk as long as they do as I say.'

Margaret Thatcher PM, 1980

Last Words

'When the going gets tough the tough get going'

A saying

DEFIANT PARKINSON'S TV
MESSAGE: I WON'T QUIT
Daily Express, 11/10/83

PARKINSON RESIGNS
London Evening Standard, 14/10/83

MY WAY OR I QUIT – PRIOR
James Prior, the Employment
Secretary, has made it clear that he
would resign . . . if he were moved
from his present post.
Sunday Times, 13/9/81

Mr Prior agreed to serve as Secretary of
State for Northern Ireland.
Times , 15/9/81

BRITTAN WILL NOT RESIGN
(Thatcher) said there was 'no question' of Mr Brittan resigning.

Daily Telegraph, 23/1/86

LEON BRITTAN RESIGNS

Daily Telegraph, 25/1/86

'I am the last person whom it would be reasonable to expect to leave the Conservative Party.'

Enoch Powell MP

In October 1974 Enoch Powell became a member of the Ulster Unionist Party.